THE
BACHELOR
SLOB
IN THE
KITCHEN

THE BACHELOR SLOB IN THE KITCHEN

*Gentle assistance and counsel
for persons who are retired,
are not independently wealthy,
loathe the preparation of food,
and despise housekeeping
in general.*

ROBERT MacGREGOR SHAW

BEAVER'S
POND
PRESS

ISBN 10: 1-59298-415-2
ISBN 13: 978-1-59298-415-2

Library of Congress Catalog Number: 2011931113

Printed in the United States of America

First Printing: 2011

15 14 13 12 11   5 4 3 2 1

Photography by Robert B. Shaw
Graphic design by James Monroe Design, LLC.

 Beaver's Pond Press
7104 Ohms Lane, Suite 101
Edina, MN 55439–2129
(952) 829-8818
www.BeaversPondPress.com

BEAVER'S
POND
PRESS

To order, visit www.BeaversPondBooks.com
or call (800)-901-3480. Reseller discounts available.

In memory of my wife,
who would probably be amused by everything—
but not surprised by anything—in this book.

CONTENTS

PREFACE

Right off the bat, a confession: the title *Bachelor Slob in the Kitchen* is a deceptive, tricky device to get you to read the book. I wrote this book not just for bachelors but for all persons who live alone—spinsters, widows, widowers, students, bachelors—*all* loners like me who hate being in the kitchen and *loathe* the preparation of food.

Most women will not like this book. When they read my four standard, gross menus or the happy way I stomp down the kitchen wastebasket, some women will surely be seized with nausea and rush to the nearest bathroom. There's an outside chance, though, that a few women loners might find value in my comments. After all, loathing the preparation of food and housework is a natural and logical reaction to a life that can be repetitive, deadly dull, and utterly boring—a routine that never ends.*

Please don't look for "fun" in this book. You won't find it. It's not a comprehensive manual, index, nor moral guide about how a bachelor should live. It's merely a collection of humble recommendations, borne and

---

* I have been pleasantly surprised to find that it is chiefly women—and not men—who have given me the most help in writing this book. I suspect that they experience the same hopeless, masochistic feelings bachelors do about the never-ending work in the kitchen. At the same time, I have been puzzled that not one of these women will let me quote her in the book.

supported by my own experience, which have reduced my housekeeping chores and saved me money.

I love my Midwest dialect and you love your dialect, wherever you are. In this book I will employ my middle-American dialect and idioms whenever I feel like it. I plan to use expressions like "well fixed," "putting on the dog," "sissified," and "making me sick to my stomach." I will use the word "icebox" instead of the effete "refrigerator." I will bow to modern usage, though, concerning "dinner," "supper," and "lunch." I was taught that "dinner" meant noon, "supper" meant evening, "lunch" was what one carries in a lunch-pail or sack, and "luncheon" was what ladies do, mostly church-ladies. I surrender. "Lunch" will mean noon; "dinner" evening; and "supper" will not appear at all. Most of my readers will be men, so I will use masculine pronouns throughout (he, his, and him) instead of bothering with "him or her."

One caveat: If you paid for this book be sure to keep the receipt.

Your goods and your bads:

Lots of freedom, but the fact is that you're an ignorant slob.

You didn't plan death or divorce to intervene in your life, it just happened.

In your former life you were spoiled, *spoiled rotten*, by another person—it was a *woman*—who took care of you. She washed and ironed your dirty clothes, did all the shopping, paid the taxes, bore the children, performed a thousand household tasks, worked every day over a hot stove while you—you hero, you great, big Lord of Creation—went out to work in the cold, cruel world to bring home the bacon.

Until recently you lived a narrow and restricted life—restricted, that is, by "appropriate behavior." You wore a necktie. You carried a watch and a clean handkerchief. You worried about the press in your pants. You drove to work safely in the right-hand lane and always correctly, parked in the same correct stall and gave the

1

attendant the same correct Christmas bonus. You sat in endless committee meetings, correctly following the agenda. You made correct little lists that told you where to go and what to do. You went to church and listened to correct sermons. You were the soul of rectitude.

Now, though, you have come to a fork in the road. The sign on the right fork is "Complexity." The sign on the left fork is "Freedom." You, of course, are going to take your first steps down that freedom road. **There will be goods and bads, plusses and minuses, in your new way of life.**

The great big plus is the intoxicating feeling of freedom and liberation from the never-ending compulsion to think, talk, and behave correctly. Now, your only moral imperative is to eat when you want to eat, sleep when you want to sleep, drink from the bottle, eat with your fingers, avoid boring people, and never be forced to sit in another committee meeting as long as you live. You don't have to worry about the press in your pants. You don't have to follow any schedule except the small and rudimentary ones you make for yourself.

You don't have to tell so many lies. No more must you lie when you leave a party: "Oh, we had such a lovely time at your house tonight!" (*It was boring, boring, boring!*) No more must you lie about a person's health: "I'm happy you recovered." (*You look absolutely wretched. We all thought you'd die.*) No more must you flatter little kiddies: "My, what a talented little boy you have!" (*And once again you had to trot out the little bastard to blow that cursed trombone.*) No more must you sit and watch one hundred lousy pictures about a friend's trip to Timbuktu. (He: "Now, this one was taken in Florence where we spent five days in

Janu—" She, interrupting: "Oh no, sweetheart. That one was in Verona where we spent five days. We spent only three days in Florence." He: "No, baby. It's Florence. You can even see that whatchamacallit famous bridge in the background." She: "Excuse me, sweetheart. I think you're wrong . . ." You think: *Kill! Kill! Kill!*

Now, finally, you can get out of that book club. No longer will you have to sit obediently and listen to that big horse's ass talk about multiculturalism. Now you can get out of that church group where you have to pledge allegiance to correct belief. Now you'll sit in no more committee meetings! Now you can devote yourself to people who *really count* in your life: your closest friends, your old service buddies, your grandchildren, your family.

Financially, you're reasonably "well fixed" with income from Social Security and an adequate pension. Your health is good, blood pressure fine, bowels okay, no communicable diseases. You have no intention to marry.

You have, however, one huge disadvantage. You are ignorant, incompetent, clumsy, and arrogant about the preparation of food and housekeeping in general. You hate, loathe, despise just *being* in the kitchen. There's not much comfort on the long view.

Let's do a bit of math. Let's say you expect to live for ten years. That means that you will have to prepare three yucky meals a day times 365 days a year. That gives us 1,100 meals a year, times ten years gives us eleven thousand meals that lie ahead. *Eleven thousand meals!* Are you sure you want to live that long? Look out the window. Visualize the problem. Can't you see those eleven thousand meals stacked like huge Neolithic gravestones

3

reaching all the way to the horizon? If you expect to live longer, say for twenty years, it's even worse: *twenty-two thousand meals!*

You're stuck. You're going to have to buy the food, prepare it, eat it, and clean up after you eat, *eleven thousand times.* The only alternative you have—your only way out—is to study how to make better use of your time. Your mission is clear: learn how to get into the kitchen, eat, and *get out* with the least possible investment of your most precious commodity: time.

What you *do* with time you save is your business: write a novel, work for your church, read to your grandchildren, make friends on the Internet, work on your stamp collection, travel to see a nudie beach on the French Riviera, or just vegetate and watch TV all day long—*just so it's time spent out of the kitchen.*

Maybe I can help you shape up, teach you how to survive. Let's start with three easy steps.

Three first steps to single blessedness:

Avoiding the grocery store. Sponging on friends and relatives. Throwing something away every day.

First: **Stay away from the grocery store.** You can save at least one whole week a year just by not going to that infernal zoo.

What actually *happens* when you enter one of those huge, busy, noisy, razzle-dazzle establishments with its phony music and rows of cashiers all saying "Have a nice day!"?

Well, the first thing is that you forget where you parked your car. Inside, you grab a cart and proceed to wander around the store trying to find items on your little list. Let's say that you want to buy a box of dried milk. Can't find the dried milk.* Help is nowhere in sight. You walk to the front and ask a cashier to help. "Aisle five," she says, pointing. "Left-hand side." Back in aisle five you finally locate the dried milk wedged down among the buckwheat flour. Back to the front again, wait in line to pay, listen to all those heartfelt "Have a nice days," pay, and go out into that huge parking lot to search for your car.

A friend from St. Paul, who threatens to sue if I disclose her name, agrees:

Stay away from the grocery store. At my store, there's always interminable waiting. Buses come and unload older people to do their shopping. These people clutch bundles of coupons in their fists, and search in their pocketbooks for exact change. The clerks dutifully ring up current coupons, one by one, but—in cases where the coupon is old, folded, and barely legible—they must stop, scrutinize the coupon, and figure each one individually. These older people have coins in little pouches and like to count out the exact change. I die, waiting in those lines. Worst of all is when I'm waiting to pay for one or two items in the "Fewer than 10 Items" line and the person ahead of me unloads thirty items, and nobody will send the miscreant to the right line.

---

* Let us not, by the way, disparage dried or "powdered" milk. A box will last at least one whole month on the shelf. It will not get sour, waiting patiently for you to mix up a fresh batch. Savings in money? I calculate about 50 percent, but the main benefit is not having to travel to the grocery store so often. Grocery stores, I have found, are embarrassed to sell dried milk. It's not as profitable as the fresh stuff. Aboard ship in WWII I drank reconstituted milk for three years with no ill effects.

What's the alternative? Where should you buy your food? At the co-op, of course. It's the place where you can buy your staple foods (oatmeal, lima beans, and rice for the most part) in huge quantities, take them home, and store them in large, covered cans in your broom closet. If there's no co-op near you, there's generally a store *somewhere*—even in the next city—where you can make a semi-annual pilgrimage to buy dry foods in great bulk. Join the co-op! Enjoy the generous discount!

This first step by itself will save about one whole week a year. You also will save several hundred dollars a year by buying in bulk. Let us not forget the expense of running your car back and forth to the grocery store for small purchases. It costs about fifty cents a mile to own and operate an automobile.

Second step toward blessedness: sponge off relatives and friends.

You will find that sponging is *by far* the most pleasant, congenial way to eat your food, particularly good-tasting food. Sponged food always *tastes better* than that awful stuff you cook for yourself at home. Eating in a fancy restaurant is fun, sort of, but not nearly as much fun as sponging off a friend or relative. Restaurants *charge*! Sponging is *free*!

Like any other social skill, though, sponging takes practice. Mastering the skills of sponging pay big dividends in contentment and happiness. It will save you lots of money, too.

If you are fortunate, you belong to a big family* that is well-populated with women who are very good cooks. This forms a natural field for creative sponging. If you don't have family who live nearby, locate friends who live close and like to prepare good things to eat. Curry their favor. Make nice! Send them a birthday card! Invite them to eat with you at a medium-class restaurant. Prime the pump!

Some sober words about the ethics of sponging. It's tricky business. Your passion, your just plain *hunger* for free and good-tasting food can easily carry you away. Always keep one rule in mind: there must be a balance, *reciprocity*, in your relationship with the "spongee." If you get the cynical habit of "dropping by" just before mealtime without an invitation, the spongee will soon see through your trick. Make it a practice, therefore, when cultivating a new prospect to "drop by" at non-mealtimes (10 a.m.? 8 p.m.?) and *always* to bring a house gift: anything that's not expensive. (It's the thought that counts, you know.) Give three tomatoes from your garden, a magazine, a clipping in which they might be interested, a Christmas gift you don't want, an all-day sucker for the little kiddie, a bone for the pet dog—*anything*. The house gift is essential. You are priming the pump. If no water comes out, don't despair. Keep trying. Eventually it will work. They'll invite you for dinner! Breakthrough!

---

* As I am in, having a number of sisters and daughters-in-law in my family who feel sorry for me. They express this by plying me with food. I am doubly blessed in having a son who loves to make, freeze, and store soups. Whenever I visit him he plies me with this frozen stuff in plastic containers. I also have a brother-in-law who loves to make bread. I am happy to say that I am on excellent terms with both my son and my brother-in-law.

At dinner you will be expected to perform. Your hosts, even those in your own family, expect you to be *interesting* and *upbeat* when you come to their house. You will be expected to make conversation, *interesting and happy* conversation. Review your jokes. Buy a collection by Henny Youngman; memorize some good ones and have them ready to deliver. If your hosts are Republicans, bone up on taxes. If they're Democrats, focus on the unemployed and FDR. Of course, smile all the time. If you scintillate, they'll invite you back.*

When sponging, always take off your shoes. The hostess, standing at the top of the stairs, will object (this is a familiar Midwest routine): "No, no, no! Don't take them off. . . ." (with, perhaps, a self-deprecating comment) "It won't make any difference in *this* house." Ignore her. Bend over painfully and take your shoes off, saying something like "No! Not in your nice house." This will pay off later. Hostess to husband: "Oh, he's so nice and neat! He just *insisted* he take off his shoes."

You don't save much time in sponging, but you certainly save a lot of money. Three ears of corn from your garden or a clipping from a magazine in exchange for a thirty-dollar gourmet dinner is a very good deal indeed.

---

* In discussion with a fellow bachelor I have learned of a different and contrary strategy, one I believe to be absolutely false: Make them feel sorry for you. Wear ragged clothes, he says. Cultivate the lean and hungry look. Quote Sartre, Nietzsche. Break into tears from time to time. That strategy may work short-term, but will quickly wear itself out: They'll see through your dirty little trick and you will not be invited back for dinner. They'll just put out a crust of bread. No: Your host and hostess want to be entertained! Everybody wants to be entertained!

Third step: Minimize!

Celebrate every day by giving away, selling, or junking at least one item from your inherited pile of stuff.

The first things to junk are schedules. Making little lists for yourself should be regarded as nothing but a bad habit: Lists, schedules, routines are precisely what you want to *avoid, to get away from*! Make no dirty little reminders that force you to do certain chores *at a certain time*: wash clothes on Friday, not Thursday; wash dishes immediately after you eat; write thank-you letters for every invitation or gift, on and on. *Schedules kill your spirit!* Without schedules, each day is a different story punctuated by new questions and happy surprises! There are, however, a few *principles* you should follow (the Golden Rule of Polite Dinner Conversation, the Principle of Food Miscibility, and the Principle of Food Enhancement), but these are basic guides to behaviors that are in force *all* the time.

Learn the joy of slimming down, minimizing, cutting down on, reducing piece by piece that pile of physical junk in your house. Celebrate every day by giving away, selling, or throwing away at least one item from that huge stock of flotsam and jetsam. There are supposed to be about thirty-five thousand items having corporeal substance in the average American house. You've got a long way to go. Reduce the pile! Think: *What can I give away today?* You can, by the way, use many items for house gifts when you go out sponging.

You have a complete table setting for twelve persons; they've been sitting there on a top shelf for many months. Do you think you will ever host a dinner for twelve persons? Come on, you selfish pig: Give those plates and silverware to someone who will *use* them, like your granddaughter, your niece, or the daughter of a friend who is getting married. They *need* those place settings! Get rid of surplus dishes, glasses, and silverware, too! Minimize your stock of furniture. Do you need fifteen chairs? Do you need that dining room table with six leaves? Do you need all those books? Give them to your local library! Don't kid yourself—you will never read them again. Keep Shakespeare, the Bible, the family archives, photos, old letters, and documents—only what you will read again, review, and cherish.

Minimizing will not save you time. Except for tax deductions, it won't save you money. It will pay off, though, in a leaner, unburdened way of life. As you watch your estate shrink to reasonable proportions you will experience a warm, snug feeling as you walk down the bachelor's road to bliss.

Dismantling kitchen appliances is wonderful fun. Let's start with the dishwasher. Unplug the damned thing. Use it only for storage. You don't *need* it. The motor—count on it!—will go kaput once or twice a year and each time it will cost eighty-five dollars to get it fixed. An empty dishwasher is an excellent place to store all sorts of kitchenware.

The oven: Don't use it except for storage. It's a great place to keep your big iron frying pan and soup kettle. An oven is spacious and it's at the right eye level. If it weren't for occasionally frying eggs and potatoes and making toast, you could throw the stove out, too.

The food compactor. Do the same: Disconnect it! Another thing to go wrong! All you need to keep your kitchen sink drain open—and abort those one hundred-dollar calls to your plumber—are (1) a small, round plug with a screen to catch food bits and debris and (2) a regular dose of Drano. Keep a close eye on what goes down the drain, especially food scraps. It is said that fatty stuff tends to stick to the inner lining of a drain, eventually blocking it. Clear this stuff out with Drano. Read directions! It's powerful stuff!

Now (this one is fun!) throw out your toaster. At least once a year that rickety device will not work, and once again you will spend hours locating a repairman, taking the toaster to and from his shop, and shelling out another seventy-five dollars. Toasters, you know, sometimes cause house fires: Oily crumbs collect at the bottom and can break into flames. Safety first! Throw that cursed thing away. With a bit of practice you can make reasonably good toast on your big iron frying pan. Yes, it works! Turn to medium heat, squirt a few drops of oil in the frying pan, put a slice of bread directly on the oil, be sure to stick around, and every minute or so turn the slice over. Beautiful toast!

Without hesitation, throw out that coffee-maker. There is a better way, the old-fashioned way, to make better-tasting coffee. Let's say you want to make two cups of coffee. Turn the stove burner on full, pour two cups of hot water into a small saucepan, put saucepan on the stove, and bring to a boil. Add three teaspoons of coffee. Let the mixture boil for about forty-five seconds. (Don't go away! It could boil over!) Remove, let mixture simmer down, and pour directly through a hand-held strainer into a cup. Don't put the grounds down the drain: shake them carefully into the kitchen wastebasket. Both methods take about the same time to prepare, but the old-fashioned system, in which coffee is actually *boiled*, makes stronger and better-tasting coffee in my opinion.

Keep your cell phone, but disconnect the other one. You can also junk your answering machine in the bargain—two for one! Always take the cell with you when you go out, but remember to plug it in when you get back. You'll need it if you get lost or have a flat tire. A cell phone is *convenient*. If you keep it in your shirt pocket you don't have to get up and walk across the room to answer a call. Remember, though, only three places for the cell: shirt pocket, top of the dresser, or plugged in while being recharged.

Now the big one: Throw out that television set. Now, I am not saying that TV is all bad. Some of it is very good. All of it, though—even the news—is *entertainment*. TV sets, I have heard, are turned on about five and one-half hours a day in the average American home. Do you need that much diversion? If time is important to you, that monster in the corner is by far the greatest time-waster of them all. Give it to Goodwill. Go for information and personal contacts on the Internet. (When our president speaks, when our baseball team is winning, or each week when *60 Minutes* rolls around, I experience a deep craving to sit in front of that TV set. I can generally manage a TV-sponge for such events.)

Get rid of white tiles and rugs on your floor. A white background makes every blemish, every little speck of dust *stand out*! It will drive you nuts! Try to resolve this problem with the owner of your pad. Insist that anything white on your floor be replaced with something dark and patterned. There are few more maddening experiences than finding big, brown footprints all over the white bathroom rug—thanks to stomping the waste-basket containing fresh coffee grounds.

You don't need high-up shelves, you don't need low-down shelves. To see what's on that top shelf, you will stand on a rickety chair, fall down, break a hip-bone, go to the hospital, and die. To see what's on the bottom shelf in your kitchen, you will lie flat on the floor and shine a flashlight to see what's tucked away in there; while struggling to get up, you will fall backward, break a femur, go to the hospital, and die. You're stuck with those shelves. Just don't put anything on them.

You don't need bottled water. You *do?* Oh, my heart bleeds for you! Here's a poem that will help ease your pain.

Take my house, ye gods, and then sell it for a ball-point pen.
Sell my house and sell my daughter.
(But please don't take my bottled water!)

Sacrifice my Andrew Wyeth. Abrogate my balanced diet.
Live with livestock, eat their fodder. (Just to keep my bottled
water.) Evict me naked, stiff, and sore, begging handouts door
to door. Prostitute my aging mater.
(But hands off from my bottled water).

Take away Jacuzzi tub. Auction off my B-M-Dub.
Drink my claret, my Bordeaux. (But leave me with my H_2O.)
Cut my credit card in two. Trash my Facebook, iPod too. Bot-
tom line: I think you oughter.
(Leave me with my bottled water.)

Reaching high: Nothing on the top shelves, nothing on the bottom—a good bachelor's rule. Here, the bachelor stands on a rickety chair and stretches to explore what's up there. He will stretch too far, fall, strike his head, and die.

There are some things that you really do need.
You need professional mentors and advisors. They
are essential! Find a CPA to do your taxes and advise you
about finances in general, have a physician on tap to call
when you get food poisoning from that ancient stuff in
your icebox, and hire a nephew (yes, *pay* him!) who can
come in and repair things around the house. Retain a
computer expert to bail you out when your printer fails
to work and introduce you to the brave new world of the
Internet. The gourmet cook in your neighborhood: You
need him or her, too.

**In the kitchen you need basic tools: a microwave,
a Chore Boy, an egg timer, a hot pad, and an apron.**

The microwave is the bachelor's best friend. It is
so *fast*! In two minutes, *WHAM!*—oatmeal bubbling in the
bowl. In twenty-five seconds, *ZAP!*—half a cup of day-old
coffee steaming hot! In ninety seconds, *WOW!* A slab of
cheese on a slice of bread: Sandwich Celeste! (On the other
hand, four minutes on a potato that hasn't been punc-
tured, *BANG!*) It doesn't take long to learn the correct
times, measured mostly in seconds, to cook routine food.
It does take a long time, however, to clean the microwave
when an unspeared potato or an egg explodes. Water, by
the way, will also explode if super-heated in a clean glass.
The FDA warns about this problem.

The apron (pronounced in the Midwest as "a-*pern*"
with a long "a" as in "day") protects your clothing from
getting spattered with grease and food particles when
you're cooking or eating. It's better than a napkin. It
doesn't fall on the floor.

You need a Chore Boy, too. A Chore Boy is a bundle of small metal strips that you use to scrape food

The bachelor's good friend: the Chore Boy! Lots and lots of authority! Dishrags are wimpy!

off dishes and keep your sink and countertop clean. A Chore Boy has authority—much more cleaning power than a limp dishrag. No dried bit of food, no blemish nor stain on the counter, no scum on the inside of the sink can withstand one or two vigorous scrubs with that great little instrument. A sponge—even one with a rough, sandpapery side—simply does not have a Chore Boy's raw power. Keep that little metallic bundle near at hand at the kitchen sink. Don't squirrel it away underneath where you'll forget it. If you do, it will rust. Don't use a Chore Boy on your good silverware, and never on clothing.

And the egg timer? For the bachelor, this gadget is as important as a wristwatch. Let's say you're frying potatoes. You have taken your big frying pan out of the oven, poured some vegetable oil on it, placed the potato slices carefully on the pan, and turned the stove to medium heat. The telephone rings—could be your CPA! You rush to answer it. At this point if you do not remember to set that little timer, those potatoes are going to burn. Let the telephone ring while you set the timer. If you don't, if you become engrossed in a conversation with your CPA, the smoke alarm will go off. You'll rush back to the kitchen and find your frying pan in flames.*

A timer can also help you terminate a long and boring telephone conversation. If you are bogged down with a compulsive talker, make that little bugger go off. The person at the other end will hear it. You say: "Whoops! Emergency! Got to go! Something on the stove!" It's a lie, but it works like a charm. Keep that little gadget near your telephone, handy by.

Your needs for utensils and cooking gear are simple. In case you entertain, you'll need three or four sets of dishes, silverware, drinking glasses, and coffee cups. You'll need a heavy iron frying pan to fry potatoes and eggs, a big iron kettle for your soup, and a set of large plastic bowls.

The hot pad. Also an essential tool. You use it many times a day. Keep it on top of the microwave and use it to remove hot stuff.

First-aid kit. Three accidents lurk just around the corner in the bachelor's way of life: (1) Lacerations to fingers with a sharp knife, (2) concussion from falling backward while stomping, and (3) automobile accidents.

---

* Earl Lellman, a retired newspaper publisher who lives near Forest Lake, Minnesota, agrees: "When steaming foods like veggies or rice, always use a timer. As I grow older, I find it's becoming easier and easier to forget the pan that's happily steaming away—until I begin to wonder where that beeping is coming from. I've ruined two good aluminum pans by letting the water boil away that way."

Have two first-aid kits: one in your pad, the other in the car.

Clothing. Sweaters are good, dependable friends. When you travel *anywhere*, always take a sweater. When the temperature is twenty below zero just outside the window, wear a sweater to bed as a nightgown.

Here are some random suggestions that may reduce a bit of trauma.

Appointment calendar. Just have one! Multiple calendars will drive you nuts. Make your own calendars by using a yardstick and felt-tipped pen to draw straight lines; tape the calendar of the month to the front door of your icebox. Faithfully enter all dates in big, black letters, and remember to *look* at that calendar first thing when you get up in the morning.

Broom. You'll need a broom. What's a broom? It's a device with a long, wooden handle with longish fibers on one end. It is used to keep your floor clean. You grab it with two hands and drag it across the floor with long, slow strokes. With a bit of practice you can get the hang of it. Do not sweep rapidly. If you do, the fiber-ends will flip little bits of dirt all over the place.

Dustpan. You'll need one of those things, too. A dustpan? It's a device with a long handle and a flat tin receptacle on one end. Its purpose is to remove little piles of sweepings that you have gathered on the kitchen floor. Place the edge of the pan close to the pile and sweep the little piles (not too fast!) into the pan. Takes a bit of practice. Empty the pan into the kitchen wastebasket.

Keys and key rack. Make a duplicate of your car and house keys. You're probably going to lose one set. Put the other one in your dresser drawer.

Money: Cut up that credit card! Pay *only* with cash or check. Cut that dirty, little plastic thing into two pieces and assign them to their proper place with coffee grounds, eggshells, and decomposed food in your kitchen wastebasket. Paying with a credit card is deceptive. You don't *feel* money going out in the way you do when you hand over hard cash. It's so modern, so efficient, so free and easy, so deceptive—just hand it to the clerk, watch it go through the little machine, sign, put the receipt away, and forget it. Paying by cash *hurts*. You see real, hard-earned money going straight down the drain. It makes you aware of what things *cost*. Credit cards exploit ignorant people. Don't be ignorant! Cut it up!

Pay bills when they come in, don't postpone doing so with the thought "I'll let 'em collect, do them all Saturday morning." That doesn't work. Saturday comes and you have something *else* to do. When you're traveling *never* place your wallet on the counter when you're talking to a clerk. The man standing behind you is a pickpocket, and the man behind *him* is an accomplice. The pickpocket sees the wallet, and watches for the five or ten seconds when you turn your head. You turn, and ZAP! Wallet's gone. The pickpocket has handed it to the accomplice who is standing just behind him.

Pockets: Empty them as a last duty of the day.
Whenever you change your clothes or go to bed, *empty all pockets*. Put keys, wallet, and checkbook—your three most important items in the house—in their proper spots on top of the dresser.
   Next: food!

III
Coping with food:

*Basic principles of the bachelor's cuisine.
Reducing the kinds of food you eat. Reducing
meals to two a day. Becoming a vegetarian.
Losing lots of weight!*

L et's start by junking two decadent ideas about
the preparation of food, ideas that serve as
nothing but restrictions on a bachelor's life.

There are two prevailing ideas, both wrong: (1) That
foods should not be mixed with each other but eaten
separately, and (2) that foods should never be enhanced,
i.e., made to last longer by the addition of water. I hasten
to correct both of these decadent ideas.

**First, the misguided thought that one must not
mix foods.** False idea, easily disproven. Close your eyes
and open the icebox door. Grope inwardly and remove
the first two items you touch. Open your eyes. Mix both
items, even if you have to chop them up (apples, carrots,
old bread) and *taste* the mixture. See? It works! A brand
new taste! What you have discovered is the Principle of

Miscibility, to wit: All foods, with minor exceptions*, mix well with each other.

The second misguided idea is that foods should never be enhanced, or as the *gauche* say, "watered down."

Enhancement, extending the life of a food, is easy, painless, and so morally *right!* It is accomplished simply by adding water right out of the kitchen tap. Any soup can be rejuvenated, given new life, made to last a day or two more, by the judicious adding of H_2O. When the bottom of the soup kettle starts to appear, and the prospect of making new soup looms on the horizon, that's the time to enhance! Just add water, *ad libitum*, a bit of salt, and rejoice with a fresh supply of attenuated, second-rate soup! Reconstituted milk also responds generously to enhancement. When your (reconstituted) milk pitcher is almost empty, you will see a white, gummy residue in the bottom of the container. Don't throw that white scum away—enhance it! Fetch a rubber-tipped scraper, turn on the cold water, and vigorously scrub that white sludge, causing it to dissolve. Add cold water *ad libitum.*** It will keep you going for at least another day or two. Beer or wine should never be enhanced. It will spoil the taste.

---

* Some mixtures, it must be said, will bubble up and explode when mixed. It behooves the careful bachelor to be aware of these explosive combinations. Chili mixed with old oatmeal and horseradish will explode. Week-old broccoli when heated in a microwave will explode and leave a smell that you will never forget. An unventilated potato will explode.

** It has been pointed out by a lady friend who of course remains anonymous that a supply of liquid soap can be given longer life through enhancement. "I pour half of it into another container and fill the original one with water," she says.

The Principle of Enhancement: Soup, shown here in the large bowl, is being given new life.

Solid foods can also be enhanced by the addition of other solid foods. A handful of lima beans, for example, when thrown into the soup, will extend it for another day or days. Chopped-up celery (leaves and all) and chopped onions are very good soup-enhancers—in fact, chopped-up *anything* can serve to give new life to old stuff.

You don't need to eat three meals a day. You can do it with two. Under pressure, you could probably manage by eating only one, with heavy snacking.

Let's pause to consider the distinction between a meal and a snack. What's a meal? What's a snack? Well, a meal is what you eat sitting down; a snack is eaten standing up. A meal is eaten, for the most part, with knife, fork, and spoon; a snack is eaten with fingers. A meal requires forethought, planning, and intent. ("Soup again, sliced apples on the side, enhanced milk.") A snack requires no thought at all: It's just sort of a reaction, something that just *happens* when you open the icebox, look inside, seize the first thing you see, and *eat* it. It could be a pickle, a crust of bread, a chicken leg, an old piece of pie, *anything.* When you snack, you're free to walk around and philosophize, plan your day, check who's sending you e-mail, read a book, or go for a walk—*as you are snacking.* At a sit-down meal, though, you're immobilized, anchored, you can't move around. This creates an entirely different mood. When you snack, you're *free!*

Snacks almost always are eaten with the fingers, but certain foods can satisfactorily be snacked by using a big serving spoon. Peanut butter is an example. Thrust that spoon into the peanut butter jar, get a *half-spoonful* on the spoon, push the peanut butter back a bit, and load the other half with jam or jelly. Great dessert! (There's a tidy little trick you should be aware of when eating a snack that is dry and crumbly. Hold the piece of cake, or whatever, in your right hand. Hold your left hand in a cupped position just under your chin to catch crumbs and other bits to prevent them from falling to the floor.)

It's not a good idea to snack in bed. It's naptime, let's say, and you plan to prop up a couple of pillows, turn on the bedlight, read a book, snack on a sandwich, and take your nap. You make the sandwich, cut it in quarters, arrange them on a plate, place the plate carefully on the bed, and proceed to read the book. The problem occurs when you drift off to sleep. Your left arm drops into the sandwich. You roll over and squish mayonnaise all over the bed: a first-class mess. A few crumbs in the bed you can handle, but mayonnaise, no. Rolling over on chocolate is the worst. Snack standing up, not lying down.

Without hesitation, eliminate breakfast. What is there about this morning meal that makes it so complicated? Well, to begin with, there are special breakfast foods that take a lot of time and work to prepare: pancakes or waffles, for example. Even a "normal" breakfast is complex: orange juice, toast, jam or jelly, eggs, a bewildering array of dry cereals, coffee, fruit, on and on. Breakfast dishes take twice the time to clean (especially if you've eaten pancakes or waffles) than for all other meals of the day. If this is true, then why pancakes at all? Why waffles? Why that multitude of crispy, sugary cereals that come in boxes? Why go to the work of making pancake-mix or waffle-mix, spatter it all over your counter, floor, and clothes, and spend *another* hour removing those hard little spots from the environment? No. Breakfast isn't worth it. Start the day with a snack and a cup of coffee. Nothing like that first, sweet *schluck* of coffee in the morning.

The idea of breakfast is new and effete. It was unknown to the Celts, the Anglo-Saxons, and the Norse invaders who all ate one meal a day. The Celts ate oatmeal and called their meal the *authogolom*. The Anglo-Saxons called their meal the *morgenfressung*. Not much is known about Viking meals. Breakfast came in during Queen Victoria's reign.

Eat two meals a day. Snack whenever you feel like it.

7–10 a.m. Snack, garnished with apple slices. A cup of coffee—perhaps yesterday's recycled brew.

11 a.m.–1 p.m. First sit-down meal of the day: Oatmeal Ennui (or any oatmeal-soup combination), reconstituted milk, side dish of sliced apples.

4:30–7:30 p.m. Second sit-down meal: Potage Celeste enhanced with chopped-up items (potatoes, carrots, celery, onions, anything). Dessert? Sliced apples go well with Potage Celeste.

10 p.m. Snack. Whatever greets your eyes in the icebox washed down with reconstituted milk. Dessert? A spoonful of peanut butter with a dab of honey buttressed with slices of apple on the side.

Pick your "core" foods carefully, and pick only a few. I have eight core foods: oatmeal, beans (lima and pinto), rice, powdered milk, potatoes, eggs, bread, and apples. Please note that my core foods nicely satisfy requirements for a balanced diet: oatmeal, potatoes, rice, and bread give me carbohydrates; beans (lima, pinto) and eggs supply protein; and apples furnish vitamins, minerals, hormones, enzymes, and antibodies. I get vitamin D from the sun.

These staple foods are nutritious, and can be stored for weeks or months in your icebox or broom closet. I have found that after six weeks or so, potatoes shrink a bit, and some of them will get soft and rotten. Apples also tend to shrink up and rot, but it takes longer. The

Enough oatmeal for a year: This forty-pound bag is full of that good, nutritious, all-purpose stuff. Bugs can't get in: the neck of the bag is always tied shut and the garbage-can lid is always closed firmly in place.

---

whole potato and the *whole apple*, by the way, should be eaten. Your intestinal tract needs roughage, and potato skins and gritty stuff in apple cores are great for roughage. I have been warned that apples contain a tiny bit of cyanide, which explains the slight jolt I get when I chew apple seeds. Apples should be sliced and placed artistically in a side dish. They're easier to eat that way. It's hard to get your teeth around a whole apple.

Please note that I have not included meat in my cuisine. It's not that meat doesn't *taste* good, it just doesn't last very long in the icebox. When you store it, meat has to be wrapped up. It's also expensive. There is, they say, also a certain problem if you eat meat that is spoiled. The problem is that you will die. I have no philosophical problem, though, with eating meat at someone *else's* house. I trust them. I find that donated soup often has chopped-up meat in it.

Buy your core foods in bulk, at a co-op. If you don't have a co-op store near you, then you'll have to pay through the nose to buy smaller quantities in fancy little plastic packages from your grocery store. My core foods are also cheap. I figure that a bowl of Oatmeal Ennui costs me about seventeen cents for the oatmeal and the milk. Adding sugar and raisins makes the costs go right through the roof: about twenty or twenty-one cents a serving.

Bachelors should have a few standard menus or "core" preparations. Let us start with Oatmeal Ennui and a general comment about oatmeal—the "core of cores," the king of foods, the bachelor's delight, the fundamental staple of them all! Oatmeal doesn't have much to offer as to taste. It has no taste. What one tastes when eating oatmeal is sugar, nuts, or raisins—spices or condiments that have been added. Oatmeal, like lima beans, is taste-neutral. What it lacks in taste, though, oatmeal makes up in speed and nutrition. Oatmeal's chief virtue is that it is infinitely miscible. A left-over portion can be stored for days in the icebox, taken out, and mixed with all kinds of things. It can become part of Potage

Celeste, acting as a sort of glue to hold chopped-up elements in place. It can be mixed with miscellaneous bits, fried with an egg, and served as crisp little patties to delighted guests. It can be eaten at any time of the day or night. It will "keep" for a long time in the icebox, at least for thirty days, after which it tends to become very hard and turns green. Viva oatmeal!*

After some experimentation I have concentrated on four standard menus. They all have French names. (Any food, you know, tastes better if it has a French name.) My four favorites are Oatmeal Ennui, Potage Celeste, Sandwich Surprise, and Omelette Formidable.

Let us start with Oatmeal Ennui. Oatmeal Ennui is easy to make: Just put a big handful of oat flakes into a bowl, add several chugs of reconstituted milk, a few raisins, and microwave it for no more than ninety seconds. Do not, though, microwave for more than ninety seconds! More than that will convert that good, mushy stuff into an impenetrable substance hard as roofing material. Looking for a good side dish? Sliced apples go very nicely with Oatmeal Ennui.

Potage Celeste, again, is a simple and honest preparation but hard to describe because it's always changing. It's a sort of thick soup, consisting of a nucleus of a legitimate, donated soup to which lima or pinto beans, leftover oatmeal, or any miscible stuff in the icebox have been added. To prepare, mix core soup and icebox jetsam,

---

* At the same time, it must be restated that oatmeal is absolutely tasteless. What you taste when you eat oatmeal are items you've added. The same goes for lima beans. The two of them—oatmeal and lima beans—therefore are perfect vehicles for enhancing, and not interfering with, other more tasty elements in the Potage.

enhance with water and salt, then heat for one minute in the microwave. (Salt and pepper are the only two seasonings you need for Potage Celeste—or any preparation in your kitchen, for that matter. All other spices will rot.) If you're stuck for a side dish, consider sliced apples.

Sandwich Surprise takes a bit of work. Cut a thick slice of bread. Upon this place a rather thick slice of cheese, any kind of cheese. If you have onions, chop one up and sprinkle a small handful of the chopped bits on the cheese. Salt the mess and heat for no more than forty-five seconds in the microwave. Let cool. Watch out! Hot cheese will burn you! Stuck for a neat side dish just loaded with vitamins? Sliced apples will never let you down!

Omelette Formidable is a standard bachelor's menu but it takes a bit of work. It's the menu that allows you to "show off" your skills as a chef. First, crack several eggs (two per guest) into a mixing bowl and stir them up (eggs, not guests). Do not become distracted by friendly conversation: Keep your mind on what you're doing. From the icebox retrieve anything choppable, preferably bits of meat. Chop it up, fry in a small frying pan for about five minutes, then pour those crackling bits into the bowl with the stirred-up eggs. Make one omelette at a time by pouring part of the eggy mixture from the bowl into the frying pan over medium heat. Wait about a minute and carefully turn the eggy stuff over with a spatula. It's a critical moment. If everything holds together as you flip, you've got an omelette. If it doesn't, you have a sort of miscellaneous hash and your guests will laugh at you. Season with salt and pepper and serve with (yum, yum) sliced apples again. There's a lot of show-business in making Omelette Formidable. Light candles before you serve. Wear a *toque blanche*.

Watermelon Achtung is a great summer menu to serve poker-playing pals. Preparing it is easy. Get the biggest watermelon you can buy, cut a quarter-inch hole in the top of it, and pour a fifth of bourbon whiskey through a funnel down into the melon. Let it season for an hour or so before cutting and serving. Don't tell your pals about the booze; let them find out for themselves. Watermelon Achtung at times presents a problem: the possibility of a food fight. This event generally starts innocently enough with guests flicking watermelon seeds at each other but quickly degenerates into uncontrolled laughter, the hurling of rinds, and the consequent danger to anything breakable in your apartment. A minor problem is that when flicked, watermelon seeds will stick to walls and ceilings.

I do not recommend fried potatoes. They take too long to make and the process is too complicated. After you have gone to all the work of slicing a potato (skin and all, of course), you turn the stove heat on to medium, carefully place the slices in the pan (with a few drops of vegetable oil), set your little egg timer for fifteen minutes, and retire to the front room to read the paper. When the buzzer goes off, you rise, go to the stove, and turn the slices over, retiring again to your newspaper. This time, though, you forget to set the timer. You are reminded of this mistake when the smoke alarm goes off and the frying pan catches fire. Not worth the trouble. Fried potatoes taste good, though, at someone else's house, and you know what goes well as a side dish, don't you?

There are three main sources for a bachelor's food. First, core foods bought in bulk at the co-op; second, food donated by friends and relatives, mostly soups in plastic containers; and third, food eaten at someone *else's* house. Outsourced food prepared by friends and relatives is always preferable. It not only tastes better, but it's free and takes no time for you to prepare.

Your local co-op is the best place to buy core food in large quantities. If you don't have a co-op, it's worth your while to find one—even if it's fifty or sixty miles away—where you can go to get, for example, seventy-five pounds of lima beans or a fifty-pound bag of oatmeal. Donations of food from persons who feel sorry for you are also an important source of food. If you're lucky, as I am, you come from a big family. Women in this family, some of them, are very good cooks. They feel sorry for you, and the way they express it is to ply you with food—soups, mostly—and all sorts of sweet stuff: cake, pie, cinnamon rolls, jellies and jams, even ice cream. The most important source of all is food obtained by sponging, which we have already covered.

Farmers' markets are another good food source. Isabel Shaw, a college student in Portland, Oregon, loves farmers' markets. "It's *fun* to go there," she says.

There are other possibilities. Nels Miller of Gregory, South Dakota, advises bachelors to keep a close eye on church sales. "They have fantastic food," he says. "They don't care if you belong to their church. Just walk in, pay a buck or two, and load up." A friend who wishes to remain anonymous claims that Christmas is a time of year when lots of delicious free food becomes accessible. In places where people gather, often the ladies put good-tasting stuff out there, free for the taking. A woman friend, who wishes to be anonymous, claims that some holiday tables are better than others. "If you see carrot sticks on the table," she says, "just leave! Those people don't have the Christmas spirit! Go where they're serving rum balls."

That pretty much covers food preparation. Here are a few nuggets of miscellaneous wisdom. No extra charge.

Baggies, yes! Whenever you "eat out," do not be embarrassed to ask for a bag or box to take excess food home. It's not necessary to take your own bag along with you. All restaurants have them.

Bananas. Don't store them in the icebox but put them on top of it. If they get soft and mushy, a Minneapolis friend claims that banana mush can be transformed into delicious banana bread. When I get a donated banana and it gets mushy, I prefer to spoon out that good stuff and spread it on my morning Oatmeal Ennui. M-m-m-m!

Blender, advantage of. A dear friend, who says she'll sue me if I print her name, swears by blenders. "Cutting up fruits and vegetables is arduous," she says. "A blender can save you lots of time and effort. Throw items into the blender, swirl it, and you get a soup-like mush. You can drink it right out of the blender!" What she says may be true, but a blender is just another gadget that's hard to clean and is likely to go kaput.

Booze. Have it in the icebox, but don't drink it unless you are with other people. If poker-playing friends come, break out the beer. If women come, offer wine. But don't kid yourself about the danger of booze close at hand. If you take a nip here and there—a "day-brightener" in the morning, an "aperitif" before each meal, a "nightcap" before you go to bed—you could be on your way to a most miserable end.

Broccoli. I have been advised that over the course of a day or two, unrefrigerated broccoli will emit the foulest of odors. The only time to be concerned about food odors (emanating most often from the kitchen wastebasket) is during a summer heat wave. An anonymous bachelor friend claims that he is never concerned with odors from the icebox. "I just keep pushing food back in there," he says, "and when I smell something I know it's spoiling."

Bread, old. You can soften up a hard slice of bread by sprinkling it lightly with water and microwaving it for fifteen to twenty seconds. Voila! Fresh bread! No longer than twenty seconds, though.

Cans. No canned food in your kitchen! No searching for the can opener, no struggle to open the damned thing, no danger of lacerating your foot on a jagged lid when you stomp down the wastebasket.

Cheese. Melted cheese just out of the microwave on a Sandwich Surprise will burn your fingers.

Desserts. Except at Christmas, when people give you lots of sweet stuff, don't stock up your icebox with cookies, cake, ice cream, and good-tasting stuff. Don't allow them in the house! Those sugary things will always be right there close at hand singing their siren song, beckoning, and in a short time you will weigh fifty pounds more than you did. You will get sufficient sweet stuff when you go sponging out there in the civilized world.

Icebox, exploration of. One of the great features of the icebox is this: There's always a surprise in there! When you look into your icebox you normally view it from a standing position—looking *down* at an acute angle. You can't *see* what's hiding back in there. Now and then, therefore, get down on your knees and look straight in. You'll almost always find food, like a desiccated fruitcake from last Christmas (but still good!) tucked away on one of the lower shelves.

French fries, resuscitation of. Few leftovers are more discouraging than a mess of limp, flabby, gummy French fries. You can bring them back to life in a marvelous way by shaking a bit of salt on them and microwaving the mess for no more than a minute.

Lima beans. They must, of course, be soaked overnight and then boiled. Don't boil them longer than one hour. If you do, they will get mushy. You want them to keep their shape. Rice and pinto beans, too, must be soaked before cooking. One of the advantages of lima beans is that they are absolutely tasteless, which makes them a perfect vehicle, like oatmeal, for mixing with anything else.

Multi-tasking with a frying pan. It's possible, I have discovered, to fry eggs and make toast at the same time in a large frying pan. Turn the heat on high. Squirt

Three steps at the same time! Eggs, potatoes, and toast happily commingling in the pan!

a few drops of vegetable oil into the pan. Tilt the pan so the eggs, when you break them, run down to one side. Place a slice of bread on the un-egged side. Don't go away! Every twenty or thirty seconds turn the bread over. In less than five minutes, voila! Toast, eggs, both prepared at the same time!

Oranges. They taste good, but they squirt that sticky juice all over the counter, on the floor, and on your clothing. What have you got against apples?

Peanut butter. Great for dessert! It's adaptable! You can spread a big spoonful on a slice of bread, flavor soup with it, or put a dollop on your ice cream. Peanut butter

Quick dessert! Peanut butter and honey in a small serving spoon!

is an *honest* food. It won't let you down. It doesn't go well, though, with coffee—makes a thin, oily scum. Buy all-natural peanut butter, the kind without natural preservatives or sugar.

Peel potatoes? Peel apples? Why? Don't do it! Eat the whole apple: the skins, the seeds, those little seed-covers, too—everything except the hard, woody stem. Some people have trouble eating the skins of eggplants and cucumbers. Don't be a sissy! Eat those skins, too. Pineapples, though, must be peeled.

Prepared dinners. I am under some pressure from well-meaning friends to write good words about prepared dinners. These preparations, I am told, come in plastic sacks, are nutritious, and are easily microwaveable. I am sure these sacked dinners can save time, but they are expensive and I would have to go to the grocery store to buy them. I refuse to do that. I get a snug feeling when I think of that sixty-pound bag of lima beans—tasteless, but secure and dry—in that covered can in my broom closet.

Tomatoes, red and green. It's a happy day in early June when your garden gives up those first green tomatoes. Use them as house gifts! Lots of people love to make a recipe called fried green tomatoes, which involves slicing, frying, and rolling (the slices, that is, not people) around in brown sugar. Don't put tomatoes, green *or* red, in the icebox. Stack them on top of the icebox or on a platter under a window and let them ripen.

Vegetable garden. It's a great source of fresh food—lettuce, tomatoes, kale, bush beans—from late June until mid-September. After planting and the first weeding—which really isn't very difficult—a garden tends to take care of itself. Garden produce makes a great gift when you go out sponging. The main problem with a garden is dirt you track into your pristine abode.

Keeping clean, within reason:

Dealing with spots. Stomping the kitchen wastebasket. Trusting evaporation to "do the dishes." Getting a cleaning lady.

L et's start with a discussion of spots.

When a woman—any woman—meets you, what does she see? She greets you sweetly and then what does she do? She immediately looks you over for spots. She does this because you're a bachelor—every bachelor by definition *must* have spots on his shirt, necktie, or suit coat, you know—and she is trying to help you. If the woman is a relative or a close friend, when she sees a spot (or a button missing, or a shoe that's untied) she will *call your attention* to it, and she will do it in public. Women don't "call spots" on other women's clothes nor, of course, do they call spots on their own spouses' clothes in public. That cultural blessing is reserved for bachelors.

Before you go out into the world, therefore, find spots on your own clothes and deal with them. It's easy.

Here's my tried-and-true technique.

Let's say you have been eating spaghetti, and while twisting those gooey strands with your fork, you've splattered tomato sauce on your white shirt. You can remove that spot—and black rings on collars and cuffs, too—without washing the whole thing or spending five or six dollars to have it "professionally" done. It's easy, once you get the hang of it.

When you notice a spot, go immediately into the bathroom, put your index finger *under* the fabric where the spot is, turn on the hot water, and wet down the spot—*only* the part that's protruding on the tip of your finger. Rub the spot with toilet soap (soap is soap, after all), take a brush, and vigorously scrub the spot until it disappears. It won't take long. Rinse the place where the spot *was* (not the whole shirt) and hang the shirt up in the bathroom. While you're at it, eliminate those black rings around your shirt's collar and cuffs, using the same technique. If you're pressed for time, it's possible to put on a shirt with a wet collar; within half an hour the heat from your body will dry it completely.

There is great satisfaction, by the way, in this process of removing spots. You not only have a clean shirt (tie, even pants) again, but you saved five dollars (plus three or four more dollars for your car's gas and oil) by doing it yourself. Do not fall for that useless charade of taking clothes to the cleaners.

Some stains, though, resist this bathroom technique. One of the worst is when a stain from a slice of beet, fresh from your garden, flips off your plate and lands on your light-brown summer pants. Right away you must get some water on that stain to prevent it from getting

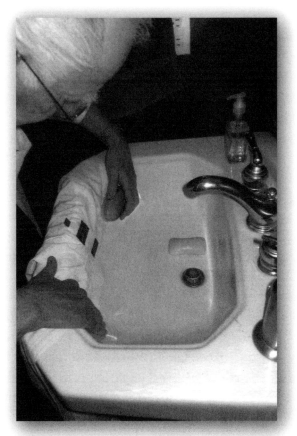

Black rings on collars and cuffs: These can be swiftly removed by scrubbing in the bathroom sink. This white shirt will be rinsed, hung up to dry, and be ready for action within an hour or so.

"set" in the fabric. If you delay, it means an expensive trip to the cleaners. Grapes also give a bad stain.

Avoid the iron and the ironing board. Do not learn how to iron clothing! Let somebody *else* do it, if at all! People in your family want to teach you how to "do the ironing" to keep that crease in your pants nice and

43

straight and your shirts wrinkle-free. Don't be deceived! *Ironing shirts is unnecessary!* If you carefully remove a shirt from the washing machine and hang it over the shower curtain, in a little while it will dry almost *wrinkle-free!* Under no circumstances should you *ever* waste your time, or the cleaning-lady's time, by ironing handkerchiefs, socks, or other little stuff. Wash those things in the bowl and hang them over the shower pole to dry. If you faithfully hang up your pants every night, the press will stay for a long, long time.

Electric irons sometimes cause fires. That's a good and necessary reason (safety first!) why you should consider bequeathing both iron and ironing board to the Salvation Army.

That covers keeping your clothes clean and tidy.

Your pad, though, is filthy. Your problem is that you're not able to *see* that it's filthy.

Do you think it's clean? Look again! Get a flashlight, bend down on your knees under the kitchen sink, and peer into the corners. There's sort of a curve of dirt in that corner, right? An old cigarette butt from a former resident, perhaps? Paper clips? Sticky stuff? Your bathroom, is it clean? Go there, take a credit card and scrape a bit on that dusky ring about four inches from the inside top of your bathtub. Sticky stuff collects on the card, right? Under a microscope you'd find that the collected goo is dirt held together by a several generations of decomposing skin cells.

You have a pair of heavy woolen socks that you have been wearing most of the winter. Do you think they are clean? Run some warm water (not hot!) in the bathroom sink, rub both socks with toilet soap, and let them soak overnight. In the morning run fresh water into the sink, vigorously rub the socks and rinse. You will see a very dark fluid coming out of those socks. It will take another soaking to get them clean.

The kitchen—is it clean? Another challenge: Take a clean paper towel and swipe it across the top of any appliance, shelf, or cupboard. Look at the paper towel. Clean? Face it! Your place is filthy, crawling with microbes. You don't only lack the skills to keep your pad clean, you don't have the *mind* for it, the *perception*. You can't *see* the dirt.

Steel yourself! Get a cleaning lady to come in once a month. Give her a bonus if she irons your clothes and bakes bread, a bigger bonus if she cleans your icebox. If you are supposed to clean it, *nobody* will clean it and soon there will be little crawly things in the vegetable bin. Don't forget an extra gift to the cleaning lady at Christmas. Your only problem with her is that she will try to "tidy up" and put things in wrong places, but you can live with that. Teach her how to stomp the kitchen wastebasket.

Keep your pad clean, within reasonable limits, by following good, productive habits. After you eat a sit-down meal, have the courage to look under the table for bits of food that have somehow fallen on the floor. From time to time (not on a regular schedule!) go to the broom closet, get the broom and dustpan, and remove these food bits by sweeping them into the pan and emptying them into the wastebasket. While you're at it, take a couple of sweeps across the kitchen floor even if it doesn't *look* dirty. It's not necessary to do this every day. Don't even *think* about cleaning that Oriental rug in

Sweeping the floor: This photo shows the correct way to sweep the kitchen floor. With his right hand, the bachelor firmly holds a broom; with the left, he grasps a dustpan. His objective is to sweep the debris into the pan and then empty it into the kitchen wastebasket. This won't work, though, because the bottle is too big for the dustpan. He will bend over, reach down, try to grasp the bottle, slip, fall backward, strike his head on the floor, and die.

your living room. Let the cleaning lady handle that with the vacuum cleaner.

You can save at least three days a year—and have a lot of fun, too—by stomping down your kitchen wastebasket. If, in your ignorance, you have been emptying it every day, you're wasting a lot of time. Ready to learn how to stomp? Here's how you do it.

You have three wastebaskets: in your bathroom, working desk, and kitchen. Once a week, consolidate garbage by emptying the smaller ones into the large one in your kitchen. Your kitchen wastebasket should be big and tough—about thirty inches high, wide but not tapered at the bottom.

Approach the wastebasket, and with one hand (your left hand most likely) grasp something solid—a handle on a kitchen cupboard, for instance. Lift one foot (your right foot if you are right-handed, left foot if you are left-handed) and place that foot carefully straight down in the center of the receptacle. Now, holding firmly to an object, any object that is firmly anchored to the building, shift all your weight to that foot in the garbage. Stand erect and stomp several times, jumping vigorously straight up and down, putting your whole weight on that foot in the garbage. As you stomped, you experienced— did you not?—a warm feeling of accomplishment. I *talk* to my wastebasket as I stomp: "Take that! And THAT! Get DOWN!"

Correct stomping technique involves some dos and don'ts. Your stomping shoe, particularly if it is a big one, can easily become wedged solidly in the wastebasket. If your foot is stuck, and you lose your grip and fall backward, your stomping days will come to a crashing

Stomping the wastebasket: The right and the wrong ways to stomp a waste-basket are shown by these two photos. The man on the left is doing it incorrectly; he is unanchored. When the wastebasket slips and falls to the side, he will have nothing to prevent his own fall. He will strike his head on the floor and die. His body will not be discovered for a long time. The man on the right is doing it correctly: grasping an immovable object for stability.

end. You will break your pelvis, go to the hospital, get pneumonia, and die. Be sure, therefore, that you have a big, wide wastebasket. Correct technique also demands that after every stomp session you should sit down, take off your shoe, and examine the sole. If you don't do this, you will track fresh coffee grounds, egg shells, and decomposed food all over your house. The shoe may *look* clean, but don't take a chance. Hop over to the sink, squirt a drop of soap on the sole, scrub it, and let it dry.

The contents of wastebaskets, after all, are greatly

compressible. Most of what's in the average kitchen wastebasket is paper of various shapes and thicknesses, broken dishes, other flotsam glued together by decomposing food scraps, and old coffee grounds. All this can be squeezed into a small, tight package by stomping. If you stomp faithfully every day, it will increase the basket's mass so that—surprisingly—by the end of one week the wastebasket will weigh forty to fifty pounds.

This creates an issue: Should you use those flimsy plastic bags to line your wastebasket? I come down in favor of the liners. In my anti-liner days I spent much time at the kitchen sink, scrubbing brown, organic stains from the inside of the receptacle. In spite of the time you waste trying to *separate* those filmy little buggers, I favor the liners: They make it much easier. A caution: On emptying day *always*, when lifting a full sack of garbage out of the wastebasket, put one hand underneath the sack to support it as you lift. If you don't, there's a fair chance that flimsy bag will break and spew garbage widely around the room, causing a long cleanup and much trauma.

Two counter-indications: (1) Never stomp with bare feet. You could easily lacerate your foot on broken dishware or light bulbs, become infected with a twisty spirochete, go to the hospital, and die. (2) During a summer heat wave it's wise to empty the wastebasket more often: two times a week. Regular stomping of the wastebasket for your legs and daily opening of junk mail for your forearms are all the physical exercises you need.*

"Doing the dishes" *a la bachelor* is a great way to save time.

---

* No better authority than St. Paul himself said it in 1 Timothy 4:8, St. James version of the Bible: "Bodily exercise profiteth little."

Let's pause to consider the old-fashioned way of washing and wiping kitchen gear.

It involved two persons. The first person gathered the dishes, carrying them to the sink, separating silverware and glassware in two neat little areas. He or she then scraped excess food into the wastebasket, using a rubber-tipped scraper. At the same time, the second person filled two pans with hot water and placed them in the sink. Water in the left compartment was supposed to be *very* hot. Person number one shook some soap flakes into the right-hand pan, making a nice, warm suds and then, using a sponge or cloth, proceeded to wash each item—first, the glassware, then the silverware, finally the pots and pans. All items were then submerged in the hot water of the left-hand pan. The second person then took a clean, dry towel, carefully fished each item from the hot water, wiped it, and placed it carefully in its proper place in the kitchen cupboard or drawer. All this took place in the context of the exchange of much gossip between the two persons.

It was a social event! And it took a lot of time—let's say ten minutes after each meal, a half hour every day. This would come to four or five days a year. Think about it: *four or five days just to do the dishes!* The modern housekeeper, though, doesn't do it this way: She scrapes leftover food down the drain and loads eating gear into the dishwasher ... and there those dirty dishes will stay, and stay, and stay until Thanksgiving when she'll have a full load.

You can perform this crummy little task in less than a minute. Gather the dishes—it's easy, you have only one of each utensil, one of each dish—turn on the hot water, and let it flow over the item. Then place it tenderly in a dish rack in the sink and let evaporation take over. That's all! Walk away! Don't "put away" those eating items in the cupboard or in a drawer. Load them in a rack and let Mother Nature do the rest.

It's probably best to use soap, but chiefly for glassware. For other eating gear, hot water and evaporation will generally do the trick, but hot water by itself won't get glassware perfectly clean. Use soap. If you put just a soap-drop in every glass and rinse with hot water, when the glass dries it will glisten. This is important if women come to visit you in your apartment. They'll be on the lookout for spots and surreptitious dirt, and when you're out in the kitchen bending over a hot stove they will hold up a glass to the light. If they see a thin film or *blemish of any kind* on the inside of the glass, *Aha!* they will think. *Suspicion confirmed! A slob after all!*

May I offer a few random thoughts about keeping clean?

Bed sheets. There is no reason why you should wash bed sheets once a week or once every two weeks.* Let your conscience be your guide. The same goes for your laundry. Do it whenever you have a load, no fixed schedule.

Dusting—never! I totally agree with my anonymous bachelor lady, the one who threatens to sue if I disclose her name: "Of all housekeeping tasks, this is the most miserable, mindless of chores. Don't bother to dust! If guests come, turn on low-wattage light bulbs."

Gardens and gardening cause big cleaning problems. If you are a gardener, you get down on your knees

---

* Or once every three weeks. Or four.

to sow those little seeds, "thin out" extra plants, or pull weeds. All this causes dirt to "cake up" on your pants and the bottom of your shoes. There's no alternative: Take off your shoes immediately after entering your pad and hang up your work clothes in the broom closet.

Frying pans give a special problem because of the accumulation of vegetable oil. Once or twice a week you get the hankering for fried eggs or fried potatoes. You take out your big frying pan, turn on the heavy heat, reach for the vegetable oil, and give a few drops into the pan. When you're done cooking, you stash the pan back in the oven—giving no thought to excess oil left in the pan. After several weeks or months, a rather thick and scummy layer of oil gathers. The oil oxidizes and starts to smell. That stuff will make you sick. Prevent hospitalization. After each use, fill the pan with water, let it sit awhile, and scour it out with a Chore Boy.

Powdered milk, a caveat. Whenever you make more milk, the empty plastic pitcher must first be scrubbed with soap and hot water. Residue on the inside of the pitcher from the previous batch will hasten the souring process.

Personal hygiene. I assume that from time to time you shower or bathe. You probably don't wash your hair very often. Do so next time you take a bath. You'll be surprised to see how dark it will make the bath water.

Shampoo as toothpaste. I have been told by a bachelor mentor that shampoo, if you have it, can double nicely as toothpaste. I can't personally vouch for that. I am also informed that shampoo can function as a detergent when you wash your clothes.

I believe I've hit the high spots about keeping clean. Next, let us consider correct behavior of our bachelor as he ventures out into polite society, a more complex—and much more controversial but still very important—area.

Brushing up on your table manners:

Practicing your smile. Coping with napkins. Blowing the nose correctly. Preventing intestinal deflatus. Entertaining gingerly.

W hen you live alone you develop disgusting table manners. You pick up food with your fingers, drink out of the bottle, wet your fingers in the drinking glass, avoid napkins, eat straight out of a can, and belch or pass gas* without feeling guilty or embarrassed. These habits have been blessed by isolated practice. They have been *learned*. You are happy with them. They save time! Before you venture out into the world of other people, though, they must be *un*learned.

Why table manners, or any kind of manners at all? The answer, of course, is that manners are a network of

---

* Strive not to perform these last two events at the same time. It will cause a condition known as "acute intestinal deflatus" caused by the sudden drop of air pressure in the lower intestinal tract. You will go to the hospital, get pneumonia, and die.

rules providing the form that governs our behavior *with other people.* It makes us happy to be with others speaking the same language, to see everyone at the table eating with knives and forks, to say things like "Happy birthday!" and "How 'bout this weather?" and to smother a belch with a napkin.

It's appropriate, then, to review a few table manners approved by mentors of polite society.

No eating with your fingers. There's no doubt that eating with fingers is more efficient, but if you do so in public it will stamp you as a crude, unrepentant slob. If you're alone in your apartment, it's bachelor *de rigueur.* As a general rule, use the forefinger of your left hand as a sort of dam against which you push bits of food with your fork. (The forefinger prevents food from going over the edge of the plate.) Eating chunks or pieces of food with your fingers is easier. Say that you encounter a crisp piece of bacon on your plate that has broken into several pieces (bacon, not plate). What's the best way to get those pieces into your mouth? Balance them one by one on your fork? Of course not! With the thumb and forefinger of your right hand you simply pick each bit up and *eat it,* wiping your fingers on your apron, which is held firmly around your neck and draped across your lap. You eat anything solid the same way. Bachelor rule: Pick up solid food with fingers! Eat!

But is finger-eating *de rigueur* when you dine in polite society? I get mixed messages. I gather that using your fingers to eat crisp bacon at a dinner party is all right. What do you do, though, about that dab of grease on your forefinger and thumb? At home you'd simply wipe it on your apron. What do you wipe it on at the dinner party? A corner of the tablecloth? Oh, no! Your napkin? No. Your napkin has fallen to the floor. You have no choice: You must surreptitiously reach down and wipe the greasy finger on one of your socks.

What about finger-eating other solid stuff—say, a small section of sausage? A piece of sausage is round, slippery, and greasy. At home, you'd simply pick it up with your fingers. In public, though, you are expected to spear those slippery little sections with your fork. What actually happens? You want to avoid making a vertical stab with your fork (the hostess has her eye on you) so you make a lateral pass at it and that greasy little piece of sausage slips and falls to the floor, bouncing off your light-colored summer pants on its way down. Family dog, wise to these things, gobbles it up.

How about broccoli, cooked or raw? Fingers or fork? The jury's out on this one, too. If you cut uncooked broccoli, it will shatter in a hundred little bits. In its uncooked form it has a nice little handle that practically invites you to eat it like an ice-cream cone, but no! Prevailing wisdom says you must cut and eat what you can with your fighting tools.

What's the approved way to eat soup? Received etiquette dictates that you fill the spoon by pushing it *away* from you, not *toward* you. It's also considered proper to tilt a soup bowl forward and use a spoon to get the last drop *but never* to pick up the bowl and drink the contents. Don't slurp.

How about fruits and vegetables? Fingers or no fingers? What's the accepted way to get those little golden kernels of corn or chopped-up stuff off the plate and into your mouth? Fork or spoon? The consensus seems to be that corn and chopped veggies must be eaten with a fork, even though using a spoon is more efficient. And fruits? How does one eat a whole strawberry? Cut it in two and eat the halves with a fork, or pick it up and nibble on it daintily, being careful to avoid those little leaves? Grapes? I gather they may be eaten with fingers. Lick your fingers? *Never!*

Avoid napkins. Use an apron. The purpose of a napkin is to protect your suit coat, shirt, and pants from, say, splashes of brown gravy or butter from your fingers that get transferred to your pants. If you are provided with a paper napkin, you dutifully unfold it, place it in your lap, and what happens? You *know* what happens. *Every time* that napkin falls to the floor. When the meal's over, you rise from your chair and notice it, bend over, pick it up, and put it on the table. At the beginning of the meal you try to prevent this by sticking a corner of the napkin behind your belt so it won't fall down. You forget about it, then, and when the meal ends you rise and walk away with that white thing flapping like a loincloth over your crotch. Children laugh at you and dogs bark. Linen napkins are heavier—they stay put in a person's lap—but they fall on the floor, too. Bachelors at home should have nothing to do with this ridiculous charade. An apron will do the job better. An apron will not fall on the floor. It does what it's *supposed* to do: protects not just your lap but your entire front.

During a meal do not lick your fingers, your lips, anything. An anonymous WWII veteran from Bloomington, Minnesota, says that GIs in the Tank Corps in Germany used to lick their plates. "When we'd crawl out of a tank we were really hungry, and we'd eat anything on the plate," he says. "And then it was common practice to lick the plate. Southern guys seemed to do it better."

Blow your nose, *de rigueur*. What's the approved way? Blow it in your napkin? Never! The *soigné* way to blow the nose is simply to get up, walk around the corner, blow, and return. The sight of you blowing your nose is most distasteful. You want to spare your fellow guests from such a revolting scene, so leave the table and blow. As you return, do not smile—have a neutral expression on your face. Never call attention to the

Fancy way to blow the nose: If you must blow your nose at a dinner table, crouch low, blow as silently as you can, and straighten up without smiling or commenting.

nose-blowing: "Well, glad I got that taken care of"; don't try to be funny: "Got a bad *colt*. Raised it from a little *hoarse. Ha-ha!*" The same rules apply when you must leave to go to the bathroom. Be demure about leaving. When you have done your duty and are returning to the table, *never, never* refer to the reason why you made the trip or the relief ("ten pounds lighter") you're feeling.

What's the wisdom of leaving something on the plate when done eating? Some say it's *de rigueur*, some say no. One lady patiently explained to me that leaving a small portion was a signal to the hostess that you were done eating—that you didn't want second helpings.

Review how to handle eating equipment. Forks and spoons should be held in the hand exactly as you'd hold a pen or pencil, not grasped like a baseball bat. Motions of the hands while eating should be short and horizontal, not large and vertical. The same, by the way, can be said for arm motions: no big, loud, vertical gestures but small, lateral, subdued ones. Don't hold your eating utensils between bites. Take a bite and then put them back down by your plate until you're ready for another bite. Pick them up again, feed yourself, chew demurely, then put utensils down again, and keep doing that. The hostess has her eye on you.

Invitations, answering them. When you get an invitation, answer right away with a firm "yes" or "no." If you hesitate ("Oh, I've got so many things going next week. I'll just have to let you know.") your hostess may conclude that you're waiting to see if a better invitation will come along . . . and she's probably right.

Brush up on polite conversation. As a male of the species you have a genetic disadvantage when it comes to participating in courteous conversations. It's not your fault; it's genetic, a matter of inherited chromosomes that you, you clunky bastard, simply don't *have*. It is *women* who know not just how to talk but to *converse* with other people. At a dinner party it's women who dominate the conversation. Men talk, but they can't converse. They just sit there like bumps on logs, listen, and suffer. As a bachelor and a man, from a hostess's point of view you're a liability. You're not expected to make nice talk. You are more or less expected to sit and listen to women talk.

Surprise them! Learn to scintillate! If you have sponging in mind, you have no choice. At dinner parties, always be upbeat. Don't talk about your bachelor life; that's downbeat, depressing. That will make people sick. Don't talk about the crazy world situation. Learn to get other people to talk about what's nearest to their hearts: themselves—*their* lives, *their* grandchildren, *their* knee replacements. Always, though, avoid downbeat subjects. "I hate peas that you have to crack with your teeth, like nuts. Busted one of my dentures once on a lima bean," or "Mince pie always makes me sick," or "What's the latest about all the botulism at that greasy spoon café?"

Practice the Golden Rule of Polite Conversation. Don't think of yourself, think of the other person. Don't talk about yourself; get the other person to talk about himself or herself. In particular, get others to talk about their work—that's always a good way to get things started.

Let us say at a dinner party you're sitting beside someone you have never met before. Take the initiative. Introduce yourself and then get that person to talk about his or her work. "Oh, I don't believe I have ever met you. What is your name?" He gives his name. "And where do you live?" He tells. "And what is your line of work, if I may ask?" He says that he is a convict, just out on parole. (You're surprised but you don't show it. Other guests start to listen.) "Oh, that's so interesting! Would you mind telling me the reason you went to prison in the first place?" He says he's a cannibal. Other guests, also following the Golden Rule, join with questions about favorite parts of the human body and a cannibal's favorite seasoning. Voila! You have sparked a conversation, an unforgettable conversation! The hostess will thank you.

Here are several sure-fire jump-starters to inaugurate a polite conversation. It's always safe to talk about the weather, but always start with "How 'bout?" as in "How 'bout this weather [this rain, this blizzard, this beautiful run of summer days]?" Be familiar when talking to a woman friend (always in the presence of her husband): "How you gettin' along with that old man of yours?" Be masculine: Talk about automobiles to any man you know. "How many miles you getting on that clunky, rusty old wreck of yours?" To a man you haven't met before, start with sports. "How 'bout those Twins?" To little children: "Let me tell you about going on a hunger strike." Whenever a conversation gets bogged down, have a ready supply of short, philosophical maxims to throw in at the right time, like "Life's like that, sometimes," "It takes all kinds of people to make a world," and "It's sure a small world, isn't it?"

Practice telling lies with a straight face. You must not do it! You must not tell the truth! To the hostess: "How do you find the time to DO all the things you do?"

(*It's because you're rich, fat, and lazy.*) "Oh, these peas are done just right! And the mashed potatoes? Delicious!" (*Tasteless. Overdone. Lumpy.*) "Oh, I'm so sorry we have to . . . [*cough, cough*] go. I don't want to give this cold to anybody else!" (*I am not going to watch one minute more of your goddamn travel pictures.*) Hostess to departing guest: "Oh, I'm so sorry you had to leave so early." (Hostess thinks: *You're feigning that cough. I hate you.*)

Always be aware of the *correct timing* of your deceptive, lying remarks. Compliment the hostess about her soup when you start to eat the soup, not at dessert time. Flatter the hostess when you arrive, not when you're leaving: "So good to see your lovely house again . . ." (*Lovely? It's a mess, and if the truth be known, so are you.*) Praise little kiddies effusively when they finish playing that wretched trombone solo: "Boy, you sure have musical genes in *this* family!" (*Third time this year you've trotted out the little monster to blow that horn.*) Pour on the praise for those one hundred travel pictures. "My goodness! You folks went to a lot of *work* to get those photos!" (*Endless ego! Kill! Kill!*)

Beware of invitations to see travel pictures. Upon receiving an invitation from friends who have just returned from trips abroad, try to determine if they're planning to "show their pictures." It takes a bit of finesse to head these disasters off at the pass. Do it this way: You: "Oh, so you're back! I'll bet you took a lot of pictures on your trip!" Host: "We sure did, and we'd like to show you some of them tonight!" Now you know: *They're going to show their travel pictures!* Thinking fast, you intervene with a bare-faced lie. "Oh, wait a minute!" you say, interrupting, "Can't make it after all! Great big conflict! Got an important meeting! Sorry 'bout that!" After, you hang up, take a deep breath, and congratulate yourself on a narrow escape.

Few events are more boring than having to sit and watch travel pictures. The pictures aren't very good (many taken out of a speeding train window), and you've probably been there before. Your hosts will generally *argue* about something. He: "Well, here we are again: Verona, at the amphitheater." She (interrupting): "Oh no, sweetie. That's not Verona. That's Padua." He: "Wrong again! I wrote *Verona* on it!" She: "Well, just *look* at it, sweetie! Can't you *see* it's Padua?" You listen, and die. Your hosts often will talk about people you don't know in the pictures and never *want* to know. She: "And here's that cute American girl, that student, who we met in Florence. Remember? We both were born in New Ulm! Know the same *people*! Small world, isn't it?" He: "No, baby. Wrong girl, wrong student. This one came from New York, and we met her in Rome." She: "No! I distinctly remember . . ." *Die! Die! Kill! Kill!*

To break a social connection, bad manners generally do the trick. You have inherited certain social connections that you want to cut, sever, eliminate. Do you want to be uninvited? Just for fun wear three different plaid designs on necktie, shirt, and suit coat. Explain in a tight little lecture that the plaids represent three clans in your family's Scottish background. Use the vernacular. Say the same boring words over and over, like "You bet!"—one of our all-purpose expressions—twenty or thirty times during the dinner. Repeat "whatever" at the end of each sentence. It will drive people crazy. A sure-fire way never to see these people again is to say you feel "ten pounds lighter" when you return from the bathroom.

Another way to break an unwated social connection is by killing conversations. Memorize a few facts. If you insert them at *just the right time*, facts will deaden any conversation. Have a ready supply. If the talk is about the hosts' lakeshore cabin (they love to talk about their cabin) and things get bogged down, remind them soberly that "Lake Superior is the largest inland body of water." When you say this, smile and make no further comment. Let it sink in. After a moment of silence, if someone follows suit with, say, a comment about Lake Superior, tell them that Lake Superior is relatively shallow. Lake Baikal in Asia is deeper. Tell them there are more than eleven thousand lakes in Minnesota. Nobody seems to be quite sure about the exact number.

If the talk is about warm weather, instruct them about global warming: "Glaciers in Greenland are melting 5 percent a year." If they claim the only TV they watch is the six o'clock news, remind them that TV sets in the average American home are turned on for more than five hours a day. If they wax euphoric about classical composers, list the ones who died of syphilis: ("Horrible disease. Before they had penicillin, you know.") When you leave your hostess will thank you privately for bringing so many facts into the evening's persiflage. "We were *so pleased* to hear the history of all those Scottish plaids." Inwardly, though: *Three plaids! He actually wore three plaids. And all those facts! No! Never, never going to invite that son-of-a-bitch again.* Mission accomplished!

For people you want to cultivate, though, it's the smile. You have to do something about that smile. That

65

thing on your face: It isn't a smile. It's a disgusting gri-mace, the same sort of expression you have when you stub your toe on the bedpost or hit your finger with a hammer. It's not that you're *out* of practice in the art of the smile; you've never been *in* practice. You have to start from scratch to learn how to control those facial muscles to *make* a smile. True, there isn't very much in your pad to smile *about*, but if you want to be accepted—particularly if you're foraging for good-tasting food—you have to do something about that smile.

Every time before you go out into society, therefore, practice smiling. Stand in front of a mirror, open your eyes wide, and tighten your scalp muscles. This will make wrinkles come out on your forehead. Now draw up the corners of your mouth to expose some teeth. Voila! A smile! Hold it for four or five seconds, relax, then do it again. And again, and again. Those little tightening facial muscles convey peace, friendship. They mean "I'm not your enemy." You should always tighten them (i.e., you should smile) whenever you say "please" or "thank you." Men don't smile. They laugh a lot, but they don't smile. Life for them consists of interpersonal challenges and confrontations. Women, though, smile. That's what makes them so beautiful.

Here are some disconnected comments about good manners. No charge.

Bread, eating of. Correct way: First, break a slice into two pieces. Put one half on a little plate to your left or—if there isn't any such plate—put it near the edge of your dinner plate. Hold the other half by the sides, not grasping it up-and-down, transfer to your left hand, and apply butter. Lift to mouth. Chew. Smile, but don't talk with your mouth full.

A piece of bread can function as a sort of mop to clean up one's plate. Let us say that you are alone in your apartment, eating two fried eggs. The yolks have broken and the yellow yolk-stuff has flowed over a good part of your plate. Of course, you don't want to let that good food go to waste! The logical thing to do is grasp a piece of bread in your right hand, hold the plate firmly with your left, vigorously polish the plate, and eat the bread. Should you mop your plate if you're a guest at someone's house? My mentors do not seem to have a clear answer to this, but I would say no: Do not mop your plate in public.

Burps, correct handling of. Burps can be suppressed, literally *swallowed*. Beer drinkers know how to do that. In your pad, of course, you can ventilate any way you want, but in most public places it's better to suppress all such effusions. When you burp, don't try to cover your mouth with your napkin. It's on the floor. Use your hand. Do not comment.

Crackers, breaking them. The bachelor way is to hold a soda cracker in the palm of your left hand, smash it with a blow from a fist on your right hand, and dump the crumbs into the soup. Do not do this in public! Break the cracker piece by piece daintily and sprinkle it in your soup.

Jokes, always out of place. They're always out of place in a polite dinner conversation—not only off-color jokes but *all* jokes. Jokes, after all, are for men only. Joke-telling, jokes, even—I claim—a sense of humor, all are sex-linked. I have never heard a hostess tell a joke. For that matter, I can't recall ever having heard a *woman* tell a joke. I will volunteer to drop dead if, at dinner, I ever hear a hostess say, "Attention, everybody! Here's a good one I heard the other day about the traveling salesman and the farmer's daughter!" That will never happen. That rich that rich and wonderful tradition of storytelling, it seems, must be explored only by men.

Letters, the thank-you kind. They're important if you ever want to be invited again. Don't telephone. Take the time to write a letter, using the traditional "Dear" salutation, and mail it right away. Hostess will say to spouse: "Oh, he's such a gentleman! Look what he wrote!"

Pepper shaker, blowing on it. When nothing comes out of those little holes in the shaker, a good way to clear them out is to put the shaker to your mouth and blow on it. This generally works, but will be disparaged if you do it when other people are watching you.

Telephone conversations, terminating the long ones. There's a good way to deal with long-winded telephone conversations from aging friends and relatives. When you want to break it off, use a standard closure phrase and say in a higher pitch: "Oh, it's been so good to talk to you! Let's talk again soon!" If this does not work, *start talking at the same time* the other person is talking and keep it up until the other one stops for breath. That will probably cause her (I use that pronoun advisedly) to stop. Hang up immediately on salespeople.

Entertaining in your pad. Don't entertain in your pad unless it's to entertain your poker-playing pals. In the first place, you don't have enough chairs: You've given them away. Your pals never mind sitting on the floor. Break out the beer, put on your apron and chef's hat, and fry up a batch of bite-sized Omelettes Formidable.

In the summertime, serve Watermelon Achtung. (I have already covered dangers of food-fights inherent in that preparation.)

Your pad is no place for women, children, or pets of any kind. There comes a time, though, when you must entertain *women* in your pad. This always is a challenge. Be creative! Tell them the theme will be "Depression Potluck Days." They will immediately understand from the word "potluck" that they're supposed to bring their own food. In the invitation, stipulate Depression-era costumes. Choose a date for your party a day or so after the cleaning lady makes her monthly visit.

Every now and then, go in the opposite direction. Confuse them by putting on the dog! Go all out! Rent a room at a fancy restaurant—a place where you're expected to wear a suit coat and tie. (Stipulate this on your mailed invitation: "Suit coats and ties, please!") You can *really* confuse them if you (1) wear a bow tie—that always works, (2) order wine so you can make a loud and general comment: "It's an adequate red wine . . . goes well with sushi." (They'll eat their hearts out on that one.), and (3) daintily dab your nose and lips most elegantly from time to time with a clean handkerchief. The handkerchief, by the way, must be handled correctly. Remove it, neatly folded, from your inside coat pocket. Do *not* shake it, but keep it in a folded position and then dab gently under the nose (do not blow!). Also dab on the corners of your mouth. Return it, neatly folded, to your coat pocket. No business like show business.

Now we must consider this thing called "order." Always a problem for bachelors. Even a bachelor, glorying in his freedom, needs just a little dependability to make his life tolerable.

VI

Alles in Ordnung, sort of:

Avoiding fixed schedules. Keeping everything in its place. Cutting up the credit card. Paying cash. Minimizing physical exercise.

Fight all schedules! Try to avoid the ever-present danger of over-organizing your time. Do not fall into the habit of thinking: "Saturday morning I'm reserving for doing the laundry. Monday mornings I'll pay the bills, and I won't go shopping until I have at least ten items on my neat little list." That way of looking at the world takes all the joy out of living.

Why not just wash and wipe the dishes on Saturday? Because it doesn't work! You think that you will just let those dishes pile up in the sink until Saturday and then do them all at the same time. It doesn't work. Saturday you get a phone call to play poker with your pals. Dishes sit in the sink all weekend. You think: "I'll pay all bills at one time—every Monday evening." That doesn't work, either. Monday comes and an old girlfriend calls:

no question of priority. Bills don't get paid. Sure, you have to do repetitive chores, *but do them at no particular time.* Do them as they come along. That doesn't mean you should *postpone them.* Just do them now, not at some prescribed time.

An exception: A place for everything and everything in its place. Without items in their "places" you lose control. Everything seems lost, adrift. You keep "losing things." You waste a lot of time just looking for things.

The place for your keys and wallet is on top of your dresser. The place for your dirty garden clothes and shoes is in the broom closet. The place for pliers, screwdriver, and tools is in the bottom drawer of your kitchen cabinet. The place for your checkbook is in that little drawer on your dresser. The place for receipts is in the tax file. The place for extra keys is on the key-hook, which is screwed into the back of one of the cabinet doors. The place for insurance policies is in the safety deposit box at the bank. The place for your credit card is in the kitchen wastebasket, cut in twenty-two pieces.

Losing things. What does it actually *mean* to say that an item is "lost"? It means that you haven't put that item back where it *belongs.* If your keys are "lost," look for them in the pants you were wearing earlier in the day. If your wallet is "lost," search the inside pocket of the jacket you wore earlier in the day. If that letter from the IRS is "lost," it's probably buried in that pile of papers on your desk. Keys, wallet, and checkbook are critical items for your health and welfare. Keys especially tend to flip out of pants pockets when you're sitting in deep, squishy chairs. You can't afford to be locked out, can't afford the cost of having your car towed to the dealer's for new keys. Make duplicates, then, while you may! Remember where you put the spare set!

If you can't find a "lost" item the first time, keep looking. On the second "look," you'll generally find it.

When you change your clothes or go to bed, it's a good rule to *empty all your pockets*. Put everything—handkerchief, keys, wallet, checkbook, coins, *everything*—on top of your bedroom dresser.

Don't let food supplies "run out." If you see that the sugar can, oatmeal bag, or salt shaker is running low, don't postpone! Fill them up as you go along! If you're almost out of stamps, buy more. If you're short of beer, buy more—even though your pals won't be collecting for another week.

Some bits of miscellaneous wisdom about being "organized."

Bathtub, running water. When the temperature outside your window is below zero, a hot bath is, as they say, just what the doctor ordered. Watch out, though, when you're running water and the phone rings. In the midst of a fascinating conversation you may find water lapping around your feet.

Exercise. Use the stairs: that's what mountain climbers do before their ascents.

Pets. I love pets, I really do. Other people's pets. Owning and supporting a pet costs as much as owning and keeping an automobile.

Pockets. Whenever you change your clothes or go to bed, empty all pockets. Get everything—keys, wallet, checkbook, coins—out in the open.

Vacuum cleaner. Don't touch it! Do not even learn

how to *use* it! Leave it to the once-a-month cleaning lady.

Watch your wallet. *Never* place your wallet on the counter when you're talking to a clerk. Remember what I said before: The man behind you is a pickpocket, the man behind *him* is his accomplice. You put your wallet on the counter, turn, and *ZAP!* Wallet's gone.

And now: Romance rears its ugly head.

Coping with romance:

*Beware of match makers posing as friends.
The use of a questionnaire.*

Sooner or later it will happen. Your friends and maybe even flesh-and-blood people in your own family will try to "fix you up" with a woman. They know you. They love you. They want to make you happy. They're trying to help you.*

Here's how it will happen: You'll be invited for dinner, naively believing you'll be the only guest. When you arrive, though, voila! Surprise! A single woman has *also* been invited. There she sits, smiling. It's the hostess's sister, a bit younger than you, and she doesn't look half bad.

The thought flashes through your mind: *It's a trap!* But it may not be a trap at all. When you're invited a second time and the same woman shows up, you *know* it's a trap, the good-old mating game: Your friends are plotting to make you happy. She: "He needs a woman

---

* There are at least two idioms in our language for this match-making process: "to fix one up" and "to set one up." What we say in the Midwest is "fix up," not "set up."

to *take care* of him!" He: "Well, who do we know?" She: "Wonder if he'd go for my sister? She's alone, too. She's a *good cook*! Maybe it would work!"

Accordingly, they invite her. The sister suspects that something is up: This isn't the first time relatives have tried to get her to make some *other* bachelor happy. The hostess casually passes this off as an accident. "She was in the area," she says. "Just a quickie invitation. Happened at the last minute." That, of course, is a bald-faced lie. It's a plan, a plot. Instinct tells you this relationship must be headed off at the pass. At the same time, the sister looks pretty good. You wonder if she has a sense of humor. No sign of it, so far.

The third invitation comes, the sister's there again, and now is D-day. You have to bring this to a head. There's still a lot, an *awful* lot, you don't know about this woman and the clock is ticking. It's time to get information, time to get facts.

"I hope you don't mind," you say as you prepare to leave after dinner, "but you know, I'd like to know you better! Now, I've developed what I call my 'MHH' questionnaire. It seeks information about money, health, and a sense of humor. Here's my MHH!" (Hand it to her.) "And here's a blank one for you!" (Hand it to her.) "Would you fill it out and return it to me?"

Questions on my MHH questionnaire get right to the point:

1. **Money:** What figure do you get when you divide your current assets by your current liabilities? Do you like figures, arithmetic? Do you like to do the federal income tax? Do you like to shop?

2. **Health:** appetite, blood pressure, bowels—all okay? Allergic to anything? Any chronic diseases? (If so, list separately.) Do you snore?

3. **Humor:** Do you like to tell jokes?

She is puzzled, but accepts the form. Chances are that's the last time you will see or hear from that particular woman, but you will have saved a lot—an awful lot—of time.

There is a one-in-one hundred chance, though, that she will see the humor in it all, and will return that gross little questionnaire. The road is clear, then, for more exploration. What you're looking for, after all, is a companion: Someone to tell jokes to, someone who will laugh uproariously when you tell her a joke—and occasionally tell a joke of her own!

You may be tempted, as you go along, to move in with this woman. Fight the temptation! Do not do it! Such an arrangement would mean a return to the world of napkins, schedules and routines; of using the dishwasher and the food-compactor again; of eating food with knife, fork and spoon; and of saying nice things at social gatherings.

VIII
Closure:

A summing-up.
Applying for your refund.

So: You have read the book. Congratulations! **Did you save time in the kitchen?** Yes indeed! You stayed away from the grocery store: That saved you a whole week. You stomped the kitchen wastebasket and gained four more days. You ate four standard preparations, bought in great bulk, ate two meals a day, and saved ten more days. You enhanced all foods, saving three or four more days. You persuaded your landlord to put dark, patterned tiles in your pad and saved two non-sweeping days! Total saving: one whole month of your precious time! (If you threw out your TV set, you saved *another month*. Sorry to mention that. TV's a sore point.)

Did you save money? Yes. A lot of it. You cut your food bill by at least two-thirds, thanks to friends and relatives and a most successful sponging campaign. There were weeks and weeks when you didn't go to the grocery store at all.

Did you learn important truths about food? You did. You learned the Principle of Miscibility—that (almost) all foods mix well together. You learned the Principle of Enhancement—that all liquid foods except beer and wine can be extended, enhanced, given more life by the judicious addition of water. You learned to love the taste of reconstituted milk. You learned to snack. You learned to eat two meals a day. You learned to be a vegetarian. You learned that oatmeal, truly the king of foods, will readily mix with *anything* and that it will age almost indefinitely in the icebox.

Did you lose weight? Yes! And bravo to you! You lost one hundred pounds *just* by embracing two of my rules: no sweet stuff in the icebox and no boozing by yourself.

Did you learn how to sponge? Yes you did, but *mirabile dictu*, something else, something miraculous, happened. You started out as little more than a conman, regarding courtesy only as a way to eat good-tasting food. As you went along you practiced the golden rule— thinking first of the other person—and at first you were just pretending. You pretended you were interested in a man's work. You pretended to be fascinated by your hostess's grandchildren and her account of her stay in the hospital. You smiled, but you were only pretend-ing to smile. Slowly, though, bit by bit, other persons became interested in you and you became interested in them. People started to ask you about your work. Men friends took you aside to tell you an off-color joke. Little kiddies started to call you "Grandpa." Dogs wagged their tails when you come in the door. Instead of a cynical, lonesome old hack you became the life of the party, a caring person! You were transformed into a *mensch*, a compassionate human being, and it all started when you stood in front of that mirror and practiced the smile.

Did you throw out that TV set? If you did, you captured a lot of glorious *time*. If you didn't throw it out, but just unplugged it, the very first day you noticed you had more time on your hands—in fact, you had *too much* time! You started to read a book but just couldn't keep your mind on those words. *You had forgotten how to read!* So you plugged the TV back in: no more books, no more reading. (All that's well and good, but I have a true confession: there are times, as I noted earlier, when I get a deep craving to watch TV. Reading isn't as exciting as watching that fast-moving, fast-talking action in that violent world. And it's not in everyday black-and-white, it's in *color!*)

Did you find sweet romance? No. The sister didn't return the questionnaire. No sense of humor.

Did you have much fun? Satisfaction, yes. Fun? No. We are not put on this earth to "have fun." We are here to suffer—but to suffer with satisfaction.

We have come to the end, and now is the time to apply for your bonus. Write me a letter confirming that you have read the whole book and I will send you a bonus, the amount of which has not yet been determined. Be sure when you write that you include your Social Security number. Why, you may wonder, do I want your Social Security number? I have a friend, a Nigerian gentleman, who collects them. He has promised me a trip to the Serengeti if I help him with his collection. If you know other people's numbers, send them to me too with *their* addresses. My friend says that if I send him one hundred numbers, he'll give me a cruise around the world!*

---

* This paragraph is completely false. All other statements in this book are absolutely true.

ABOUT THE AUTHOR

Robert MacGregor Shaw lives in Edina, Minnesota. In the summer he works in his garden. In the winter he mopes. He generally avoids talking to other people. If you try to communicate with him in any way, he will not respond.